MINIMA

HOW TO DECLUTTER, DE-STRESS
AND SIMPLIFY YOUR LIFE
WITH SIMPLE LIVING

HOW TO LIVE MORE WITH LESS
BY ADOPTING A MINIMALIST LIFESTYLE

Table Of Contents

Introduction

Today, a growing number of people are becoming dissatisfied with their lives and turning to simpler ways of working, living and raising their children. This book will explore the philosophy of minimalism and how it can streamline your life, declutter your home, reduce stress and reconnect you to what's truly important.

You'll find ways to adopt a mindset that promotes simplicity and elegance in your every day life, and rethink your dependence on material possessions. Whether in our wardrobes, kitchens, work lives or our deeper sense of personal and spiritual purpose, we could all do with focusing on things that align with our values and reducing the distraction of those things that pull us away from them. This book shows you how.

Chapter 1: What This Book is About

For those born and raised in the height of our consumer society, the idea that happiness and personal fulfillment is found in *stuff* is more or less a given. The capitalist machine we all live within requires only one thing of us: that we should constantly want, and the things we should want are to be found, usually, in malls. Malls that are filled with strategically placed advertising, with the sole purpose to entice and lure you, trying to convince you that you need, not want, their specific product. Our economy relies heavily on a steady stream of consumption: better clothes, cars, bigger houses and things to fill those houses with, the newest appliances, Christmas decorations, pet toys, jewelry, office furniture, pot plants, gaming consoles, specialty tires, luxury soaps... the array of stuff is simply dazzling.

But if you are reading this there's a chance you find this overabundance just a little... exhausting. Paradoxically, there seems to be a sad sort of emptiness in filling up one's life with more things. What is simple and truly valuable often seems to be completely hidden under mountains of what is unnecessary. Although advertising tells us the best way to solve problems is to *buy* solutions, tranquility and a graceful life seem to elude us, no matter what we buy or how much of it.

Minimalism is an aesthetic, a philosophy and a way of life. This book takes a look at how deeply liberating a simpler life can be, and shows you ways you can adopt a calmer, more deliberate way of living and working. Minimalism is about clearing away the clutter that is distracting from what is really important. It's about rethinking our attitudes to ownership, to our lifestyles and to our innermost values.

This book will give practical advice on owning fewer clothes, de-cluttering your life, simplifying your daily routine and reducing mindless consumerism. It will also explore how practical changes to our surroundings can lead to a previously unknown inner peace and calm.

Chapter 2: Less is More: The History of Minimalism

One may think that it is only in our modern materialistic society that people have become more conscious of the way they accumulate possessions. But in fact the fundamental ideas of minimalism go back in time to mankind's earliest beginnings.

Ever since people learnt to farm animals and cultivate the land, they've thought of themselves in terms of what they own. And even the most ancient of civilizations have had individuals who have been counter cultural in their desire for simplicity.

Be it the ascetics of ancient India or the Zen Buddhists of Japan, there have always been those who decided that they *wouldn't* try to keep up with the Joneses. The Bible speaks about guarding against greed and covetousness, and most spiritual traditions, wherever they stem from, usually promote humility, grace and a simple lifestyle.

In the early 19th Century, artists, architects and designers felt a kind of relief in the aesthetic of minimalism. The extravagance and embellishment of earlier times fell away as people became interested in essential qualities, in the true nature of buildings, of furniture, even of music.

Today most people associate minimalism with the endeavors of these early artists, and think of the liberal use of white, of empty spaces and of sparse and elegant lines.

Minimalism is much more than an aesthetic though. Those seeking a simpler life are interested in the corresponding states of mind of clean concepts and graceful design. What these designers tried to express was a yearning many of us can identify with – the desire for balance, meaning and serenity.

Chapter 3: What it Means to be a Minimalist

Of course, there are plenty of trends today, especially in online communities that encourage people to be thrifty and save money. This is a very pragmatic response to the frankly tattered economy – families who previously could afford to throw valuable things away and barely give a second thought to the thousands of products they consumed every month were suddenly forced to find creative ways to trim the budget.

As a goal in itself, thrifty living is certainly admirable and takes a certain skill and dedication to pull off well. However, being thrifty is not quite the same as being minimalist. Making do with less because you have no other choice is merely a practical concern. The spirit of minimalism is... a little different.

To willingly do with less is not a hardship, nor a punishment. It is not some unfortunate circumstance that you endure because you have to, and it is not intended as martyrdom or a denial of the self and its needs. While a minimalist and someone who has merely gone bankrupt may look a lot like one another, they come from very different places. Minimalism is not a kind of "diet". It is not asceticism or restriction of needs, but a questioning of what one's needs really are, and willingly choosing to do with less in favor of living a more intentional life.

In fact, it is sometimes the case that people who are thrown into poverty or compromised circumstances eventually experience an enrichment of their personal and spiritual lives. Gautama the Buddha, for instance, is said to have started his long journey to enlightenment by leaving the gorgeous palace walls he had lived in all his life.

So, while many who practice minimalism in their daily lives may cultivate what others would call poverty, the goal is not to do without or to suffer. The goal is to re-evaluate whether wealth and possessions actually add any happiness, and if they don't, then what does?

Chapter 4: Hacking Away at The Unessential

How can be we bring some of the elegance of minimalism into our own lives?

Think of a hot day and the strong desire to have a cool glass of water. The heat makes a tall, icy cold drink of water seem almost like a need, in fact. While very few people in the middle class Western world ever experience a true need and the true fulfillment of that need, sipping a cold glass of water when you're parched comes pretty close. It's hot and you need just one thing: water. You pour a full glass. You drink it, relishing each drop, your thirst completely quenched. The glass is empty. This is a truly elegant process, and beautiful in its simplicity.

Now imagine a less elegant process. You're thirsty, and you fill the glass up with water, but you don't have enough. You drink it up, but you're thirsty still, and your need remains with you.

Or, imagine the opposite. You pour some water into your glass but when you reach the top, you keep pouring. You're thirsty; water is good, so more water must be *better*, right? The water spills all over the counter, and now you have to clean it up. You've wasted some, and even given yourself extra work to do.

Minimalism is like trying to find just exactly the right amount of water to pour in your glass. There is no need for poverty or denial. There is also no need for excess. Instead, minimalism is looking for that sweet, elegant spot right in the middle.

When we have too much, we have to devote more of our time to taking care of the excess, i.e. cleaning up the overflowing water. When we don't have enough, we become preoccupied with our impoverishment – which is just another way to be obsessed with material things.

For most of us, the idea that you can never really have enough is practically gospel. What we don't realize is that having extra stuff can be a significant cause of stress and unhappiness in our lives. Trying to solve this deep sense of dissatisfaction in your life by buying more is like pouring more water into your glass to ease the stress of having to clean up spilled water. In other words: it doesn't make sense.

Clutter in The Home

Here's a philosophical question: what is a home? What is a home *for*? It seems like a bizarre question, but try to answer it for yourself anyway. And be honest. Is a home a place for you to relax in between adventures in the outside world? A place to sleep? A place for your pets or your kids to run around in? Something you feel that successful adults need to have?

Probably, your answer was not, "a home is something to take up my time and money and cause me stress". And yet, this is what homes essentially are for many people. Traps. For women especially, the promise of domestic bliss, a clean, well-coordinated house and lots of pretty things to fill it with actually translates to being an indentured house servant. You may think it's efficient to pay someone else to clean and maintain your home, but somewhere along the line, you trade in your time and peace of mind in order to pay for that.

The home – the place that should be about rest and recuperation – becomes another life chore, something to juggle in the endless list of tasks that need your attention. And while you're busy maintaining all your things, do you have time to actually enjoy them? How many people in the world leave their houses empty every day to go and work elsewhere, so that they can afford those houses? Again, the question is, what is a home for?

Minimalism is not the same for everyone. The marathon runner needs to drink three glasses of water, the little child only a half. Our needs are all different, and what is important to each of us is different, too. Nevertheless, consider the following to try and streamline your home and the life you live in it.

Ask yourself what an item truly brings to your life

You bought an expensive popcorn machine because you liked the idea of having access to fresh popcorn in your home. In reality, you don't actually eat popcorn all that often. The popcorn machine becomes like the spilled water on the counter – another thing to take care of. If you accumulate enough items like this, you may think to yourself one day that you need a bigger kitchen, more clever storage solutions, or even a maid to clean everything.

Of course, there's nothing inherently evil or useless about a popcorn machine. For another person, they may use it all the time, deriving a lot of joy from making cheap, delicious popcorn at home that they share with their family.

The question is not what the value of the item is, but what the value of the item is *for your life*. Buying something expensive and thinking that the dollar amount attached to it will have a corresponding value in your life is a mistake. An expensive phone with a hundred features that you never use is just water on the counter. Does the item serve you or do you serve the item?

Decide on a lifestyle, equip yourself accordingly

If you were a single man, you wouldn't buy a deluxe baby crib with all the trimmings because you saw it on sale. It would be absurd, and very easy to just say, "Well, I don't need that."

But it's not always that easy to know when something truly belongs in our lives, and when it's just being heavily marketed to us. The same man may buy a deluxe golf club set with all the trimmings, even though, if he was honest with himself, he plays golf about as often as he cares for a child.

If you have a strong self-concept, it is difficult to convince you to buy something that you don't need. You become immune to advertising, peer pressure and nagging from your mother. You simply go out into the world and seek the tools that help you be yourself.

But if you've been told all your life that what you really want is an 8-seater dining table when you grow up, you may be confused by how little satisfaction it gives you when you actually have it. You may even wind up more confused because you're suddenly made aware of another need you never knew you had: you suddenly realize you need 8 people to sit there, 8 plates and bowls, 8 wine glasses and while you're at it, table decorations, too.

Instead, work from the need backwards. How often do you eat at home? If not that often, don't buy things to help you cook better. Don't buy things for the lifestyle you're told you *should* have, buy them for the lifestyle you actually *do* have.

Draw up a list of activities that you actually do in the course of a month. Make note of all the times you wished you had something, but didn't. If after a month you haven't used something you own, consider getting rid of it. Notice how much time you spend maintaining something and compare it with how much pleasure or utility it gives you. Is it beautiful? Is it functional? If not, why do you have it?

Streamlining Your Wardrobe

Beware all enterprises that require new clothes

-Henry David Thoreau

Fashion can be a funny thing. While people laugh at the fashions their parents followed a few years before, they dutifully follow the fashions of their own time. Fashion can be a creative outlet, a platform to express ourselves and just downright fun.

But more often that not, fashion is merely a path to pure consumerism. Most items of clothing can be worn happily for years and years. So how do you get people to buy more of it? You forbid them to wear perfectly good clothing because it's not in fashion. Buying fashionable clothes becomes analogous to buying furniture that spontaneously combusts every new "season".

With other products, advertisers at least try to conceal that they are appealing to your sense of identity when marketing to you. But with fashion, the link is clear: *the clothes maketh the man*. When a company tells you that swiping on a coat of fire engine red lipstick is what you do when you want to feel confident, they are not interested in your mental health. They are interested in selling you more fire engine red lipstick. The trick is that you can't buy an emotion or an identity in the form of an item of clothing. So you try again.

You get people who have wardrobes that are literally bursting with clothing legitimately feel that they have nothing to wear. The need, whatever it was, is still there.

Think Practically

Women's magazines tell us that every savvy woman needs a "little black dress". But if you work at a game reserve nursing sick lions to health 7 days a week, you don't need a little black dress. Forget about lists that talk about "wardrobe staples" and fashion "must haves".

Think of the items of clothing you wear the most. The ones that fell to pieces and you were sad because you wanted to wear them more. The shirt that you always grab in the morning, the pair of pants that always make you feel happy to put on.

These clothes have proven value, so take them as your guide. The pile of dress shoes sitting at the back of the closet? The expensive sequined scarf that you think is beautiful but are too scared to even wear? These give you clues as well, clues on what you need a lot less of.

Embrace the idea of less, but better. One item of clothing that is well made and fits you and your life is worth much more than several items that are sort of OK, and will only end up in a landfill once you tire of them. Try to think of where your full point is on the glass, clothing-wise.

For many people, clothing that lets them get on with the business of their lives is best. Choose colors and styles that you like, whether they are in fashion or not. Avoid fussy things that need dry-cleaning and special care, things that will disintegrate after a year or less, or clothes that take as much time to care for as they do to wear them.

If you find something you like, keep it and take care of it. If the tailoring and quality are good, it will last you for years. Invest in the extra expense knowing that what you are buying is the freedom of thinking about clothes for the next while.

Be Ruthless

Look at the closet you have right now. Ask yourself what you have worn in the last year or six months. If you haven't worn something, stop deluding yourself that you will eventually, when you have the right event to wear it to, when you lose weight or whatever. Give it away to someone who can use it and actually benefit from it.

Fix clothes that you avoid wearing because of small things like a tear or missing button. Using what you already have can be a real moment of insight. Some items can be repurposed or revived with a little clothing dye, a bit of tailoring or a good clean. Try to remember that at one point, this was a new, fancy item that you were excited to have.

Try not to let sentimentality stop you from getting rid of items that truly don't serve you. Things like "lucky" underpants, hand-me-downs from loved ones or pieces that have sentimental value need to be considered carefully. Is it the thing itself that is special, or the memory that you attach to it?

Zen Mealtimes

No matter what you do, you have a physical body that needs feeding every day. Food is something that should nourish and nurture us, keeping us strong and healthy so that we can get on with living our lives. But ask any overwhelmed stay at home mother about food, and you'll likely find that it's just another drain on resources, just another chore.

The shopping, cooking and cleaning associated with eating every day can eat up hours of your life. If you feel that eating is more of a never-ending drudgery and not something to embrace and enjoy, it may be time to pare down.

Constantly ask yourself what is truly necessary.

If you waste time chopping vegetables and get no pleasure from it, focus instead on recipes and meals that use whole or ready-prepared vegetables. Better yet, can you find meals that barely require recipes at all? Sometimes the best meals are the simplest, the lack of recipe letting each ingredient really shine on its own.

Foods like salads, roasts and finger foods require less cooking and less cleaning up. Making a big batch of food and freezing some for later essentially halves the amount of time you spend cooking. A dishwasher may be an expensive purchase, but not when you offset it against the free time you gain to relax, be with your family or pursue something that is important to you.

Emotional Eating

It's probably no exaggeration that much of the time, what we eat is not eaten to directly address hunger. Food is our most basic need, but also a very complicated social, cultural and psychological activity. We are told that heartbroken girls should eat buckets of ice cream, people who are celebrating should drink alcohol and those watching sports should eat hotdogs.

Nowhere is our understanding of our own desire more misunderstood than with physical hunger. For most, feeling as though you want to eat, as though you *could* eat, is mistake for actual hunger.

Try to be mindful as you eat. Think about your role as consumer, as you are literally consuming. Does the food in front of you help or harm you? If it harms you, why are you eating it, really? Do you *need* to eat it? Do you need to eat the amount that you are eating? Is there an emotion that you are soothing in yourself by eating?

When we are healthy and balanced, food is fuel that happens to be particularly delicious. When we are out of touch with our own needs, food becomes confused with representations of emotional states, just like products are. Food becomes a reward, a punishment, a celebration, a bad habit, a distraction, a companion, an enemy.

The goal should be to regain the simplicity in eating. Being hungry all the time or being stuffed full of food are both states that take your attention away from more important things. What can be removed? What is hindering rather than helping?

Being a Minimalist Parent

Ah, the baby shower. The parents to be are showered, almost literally, in gifts and goodies intended for the soon-to-be child. It's sadly fitting that the celebration we give to mankind's newest members is a showy initiation into consumerism. Having a baby? You need more *stuff*.

In the past, a baby shower had the very practical purpose of making sure that friends and family could help ease the burden that a new child could bring, while showing some support for the new parents. Children are, after all, expensive, and a little help is always appreciated.

But the baby shower can also be the first in a long line of occasions to buy unnecessarily. Tired parents of toddlers have houses cluttered with cheap colored plastic toys that get underfoot and are thrown out when they break or the baby loses interest.

Parents are encouraged to buy duplicate copies of everything for their little ones: baby spoons, baby brushes, baby baths, baby food, baby chairs, and baby soap. Advertisers have an easy job – no parent wants to worry that they are not doing the best for their child, and so consuming becomes a way to show love.

What's important

Think back to your own childhood. What are your happiest memories?

The moments that stand out to us even years later often have an ineffable quality to them. We were young and carefree, maybe feeling loved and safe, happy with the world and our place in it. Most likely, your memories have nothing to do with the material possessions you had or didn't have at the time. And if a special birthday present or something similar features, it's probably because of the emotions you associated with it, and not the thing itself.

Parents, especially first time parents, want to do the best for their children. But if you've spent any time at all with a two year old you'll realize that what's important to them are the little things – time spent playing with those they love, learning about something new and exciting, realizing that their parents are proud of them.

The best games don't need fancy, expensive equipment, and sometimes the game is to use your imagination to come up with something completely new out of what you already have. Even with infants, some first time mothers are surprised that their little angels didn't really need all the mountains of clothing and baby things they bought in anticipation.

Things we buy for our children can be held up to the same standard: are they useful? Are they ultimately enriching our children's lives? In most cases, the assumed benefit from an extra gadget or toy could just as easily be experienced without it.

Be aware of buying things that are actually intended to appeal to adults and not to their children. Tiny babies have absolutely no need for giant stuffed bears or freshly painted nursery walls. What they need is the warmth and attention of their parents – if buying them goodies takes you away from that, let go of the need to have it and focus on your child instead.

If you can cultivate a detached and balanced outlook on material things, you also give your children a lesson they can carry with them into adulthood: the lesson that happiness is not to be found in things.

Chapter 5: Tuning in to Your True Needs

By now, there's been enough mention of "utility", of asking ourselves the question of whether objects are truly necessary or not. But then the obvious question is, necessary *for what?*

It's strange to mention, but if you begin to live your life in a simpler way, with less clutter and distraction, you may find something peculiar happening: you're bored. You feel strangely lost. This feeling may be enough to convince you that your possessions and distractions were there for a very good reason, but stick with those feelings. They carry with them an important lesson.

The sad truth is, for many people life becomes almost completely about the management of our material possessions, the endless fussing with things that ultimately add little or no value to our lives or to the lives of others. For these people, there simply isn't anything to *do* after all the clutter has been removed. Their life is as meaningful as it ever was; only there is no stuff in the way to hide the fact.

So far, we've looked at very practical ways to remove material clutter from our lives, to stop buying things we don't need and to really enjoy the things we have. Excess clothing, toys and household junk are easy to identify and remove. But the minimalist philosophy extends into far more than this.

Human beings are symbolic creatures, and sometimes the "things" we let take over our lives are not even things at all. This is where the principles of elegance, of simplicity and of only that which is necessary can really change your life.

You may find it incredibly difficult to separate out your needs from your wants. And in the same way that we hold onto old magazines and knick-knacks from days gone by, we hold onto ideas and beliefs about ourselves that no longer serve us.

The minimalist philosophy extends to include every action, every event, every thought and every emotion. It is the practice of frequently stopping to ask ourselves, *is this valuable*?

And the answers may surprise you.

A new perspective

Unfortunately, it can take a brush with a life threatening illness or an accident for us to realize – none of what seems like it matters actually does. When you get into the habit of truly seeing what is necessary, what is good, and what makes you happy, you inevitably experience changes in your entire worldview.

You may lose motivation to do the same thankless and unfulfilling work, you may experience a whole new level of peace and contentment, you may find that you want and need to pursue something more spiritual for your life. You may stop being susceptible to manipulative marketing, you may leave old relationships and begin new ones, you may become interested in environmentalism or meditation.

Or, you may clean out your garage like you've always meant to and go on your way.

Minimalism is a bottom-line style of thinking and being that reminds us to keep aware of what's real and what's important. It's a life philosophy that recognizes that things and possessions are not goals in and of themselves, but merely tools to help us get to what's really important – tranquility, fulfillment, purpose.

The question, then, is to ask whether each activity, item or thought is directed towards your higher goals and values. If not, it is unnecessary, or worse, getting in the way of something that is necessary.

Chapter 6: Moving Forward: A Simple Life

Our time on this earth is finite and precious. We have our values and principles to guide us. Look at your "to do" list and ask whether each item truly serves those higher values and principles. You may have had the feeling before: looking back and wondering, where did all the time go? Don't throw the present away on things that don't matter to you.

Be elegant and simple in your speech and actions. Gossip, idle chatter and negative conversations only waste time and energy. Your words are also tools, and should be used honestly and intentionally.

Reduce the barrage of choice in your day-to-day life. The constant noise of news, online media, friends and family demands, movies, music, technology etc. provides an endless stream of worthless and exhausting information. Cultivate what is enriching and avoid those things that tax and dull your senses.

Instead of multi-tasking, choose to do only one activity at a time, but well. Don't be afraid of empty space, of silence or of still moments. Resist caving when someone else tries to tell you what you should find important in your life. Make it a habit to go still inside yourself and listen to your own needs, passions and sense of purpose.

Conclusion

Having a simpler life is, well, simple.

But it does take effort and presence of mind to consistently hone into that thread of value and meaning in a universe cluttered with excess stuff. Minimalism is a way of being that is counter to what is encouraged in us everyday, so you may find resistance in yourself and those around you when you choose to step back from mindless consumerism.

Start small and make slow, gradual changes that will stay with you. Deliberately open up blank spaces in your schedule and notice the effect. Choose to go quiet instead of rushing into speaking; choose to think about who you are and what you need to be your best possible self before rushing into a new purchase. In time, a simpler and more elegant life will bring you peace and tranquility, and that little bit closer to the elusive questions of truth and purpose.

Finally, I would love to hear how this book has helped you, so if you liked this book I would really appreciate it if you'd leave a review and tell me all about it. You can leave a review by searching for the title of this book on www.amazon.com.

Thank you and good luck to you on your journey toward adopting a minimalist lifestyle. I wish you all the blessings that minimalism has to offer – and they are many!

Bonus: Preview Of My Book "How To Stop Worrying And Start Living - What Other People Think Of Me Is None Of My Business"

Stress is a lot like love – hard to define, but you know it when you feel it. This book will explore the nature of stress and how it infiltrates every level of your life, including the physical, emotional, cognitive, relational and even spiritual. You'll find ways to nurture resilience, rationality and relaxation in your every day life, and learn how to loosen the grip of worry and anxiety. Through techniques that get to the heart of your unique stress response, and an exploration of how stress can affect your relationships, you'll discover how to control stress instead of letting it control you. This book shows you how.

You wake up in the morning, swatting at the snooze button and cursing the start of a new day. You're utterly exhausted, already. Maybe you fight to get the kids up, get dressed, and start the daily errands. Work grinds on you, and your partner feels like he or she is drifting away from you as your connection wavers under endless niggles and arguments about money and housework. Everything you encounter irritates and exasperates you.

It seems like every day goes like this. You race from one thing to the next, wiped out at the end of it all and seemingly never done with everything you have to do. By the early afternoon, your brain is in a grey fog and you're snapping at everyone. You can't remember a time when you didn't feel cynical and bitter about life.

At night you collapse into bed, knowing that the following day, the same cycle will only start again. Maybe you lie there and worry about getting old or sick or dying, or worry that your life is slipping past you, or about your children or your marriage. Have you had your vitamins today? Paid the credit card? Fixed the leak in the sink? Fed the dog? Gone to gym? Called your mother? Sometimes, you're not even sure what you're anxious about. You only know that the world seems hostile, life seems hard and most of the time you simply feel overwhelmed.

Stress has become so commonplace in our modern world that we are actually suspicious of people who claim not to be busy. Our lives keep filling up with more: more events, more responsibilities, more things, more people, more work. Like a bewildered rat in its wheel, we decide there's only one thing to do: *keep going*.

The consequences may not be obvious immediately, but the effects of stress, anxiety and worry are far-reaching. Wear and tear from stress can include heart disease, increased risk of cancer and even early death. Stress makes you feel awful, obviously, but it's far more serious than that. A stressed out body and mind are simply not everything they could be. Being overwhelmed cognitively means you are never really 100% available to make the best decisions for yourself. You're slower, get tired more quickly, and your memory suffers.

When you're constantly juggling feelings of stress, you're not *emotionally* available either. You're more prone to depression and pessimism, more likely to abandon projects you start and more likely to interpret things around you in a negative light. Stress also seeps into your relationships. The last thing you want to do is seek out others and be social, and this together with an irritable mood and short temper mean your closest connections become undermined.

You don't necessarily have to be a rushed-off-her-feet working mother or a CEO who's married to his high pressure job to understand how damaging stress can be to your relationships. For those of us with social anxiety, shyness or difficulties with dating, relationships with others are actually the *cause* of the stress. Low self esteem, paranoia about the judgment of others, inability to reach out to the opposite sex... Even when you manage to find someone, jealousy and insecurity sabotage your ability to relax and enjoy it. These are all just different manifestations of this strange frame of mind we call "stress".

Stress gets into your body, heart, mind and soul. Stress damages your ability to have trusting, open relationships with others. Saddest of all, stress weakens your relationship with yourself in the form of self doubt, low self confidence and bitterness. We tend to think of stress as nothing more serious than a certain tightness in the shoulders or a schedule that could be a little leaner. But stress can permeate every single area of our lives, right from the presence of stress hormones in the body's tissues to our bigger, overarching sense of who we are as human beings in this world. This book is for those of us pacing in our cages, tossing at night with heads full of doom and gloom, unable to trust those around us and the world at large. Here is a list of the ways that stress might manifest in different areas of life. If any of the following apply to you, this book was written for you.

Symptoms of Stress – The 5 Levels

Physical symptoms:

   * Frequently having accidents, being clumsy and rushing

   * Neck, shoulder and back tension. Muscle spasms and tension headaches

   * Diarrhea or constipation, ulcers, indigestion or heartburn

   * Increase or decrease in appetite; cravings for stimulants like caffeine

   * Disturbed sleep, including nightmares, insomnia or oversleeping

   * Changes in weight; weight gain particularly around the waist

   * Low energy levels

   * Acne, teeth grinding, dry skin, brittle nails, frequent infections

   * Seeking out substances, addiction and self medication

Emotional symptoms:

* Feeling overwhelmed
* Feeling sad, or like you have no hope and might as well give up
* No longer being interested in what used to excite you
* Being irritable and having a short temper
* Feeling apathetic and indifferent
* Feeling guilty and worthless
* Feeling mistrustful and suspicious of others' motivations
* Tearfulness and sensitivity to criticism

Cognitive and behavioral symptoms:

* Absentmindedness
* Procrastination and avoidance
* Being unable to properly concentrate
* Distractibility
* Feeling unorganized and unfocused, not completing projects
* Constantly negative thoughts

Relational symptoms:

* Feeling like everyone wants a piece of you
* Cynicism about relationships or family
* Loss of libido

* Low self esteem

* Shallow connections with others

* Feeling antisocial; withdrawing socially

Spiritual symptoms:

* Feeling alone in the world

* Feeling unable to summon any hope or optimism

* A crisis of faith

* A sense of purposelessness

* Feeling disconnected from others

* Feeling that life has no meaning or is chaotic

The above list is by no means exhaustive. The way stress manifests in our lives is as unique as we are and, as you can see, stress can show its face in many different ways, along any of these 5 levels. When we are in environments that are not supportive to us, when we lack the skills to adapt to challenges around us, or when we've simply expected more of ourselves than is humanly possible, we experience stress.

This book is not just another "anti-stress" book. Here, we will not be concerned with only reducing the _symptoms_ of stress. Rather, we'll try to understand exactly _what_ stress is and the role it plays in our lives. We'll attempt to dig deep to really understand the real sources of our anxiety and how to take ownership of them. Using the power of habit and several techniques for smoothing out the stressful wrinkles in our day-to-day lives, we'll move towards a real-world solution to living with less stress, more confidence and a deep spiritual resilience that will insulate you from the inevitable pressures of life.

This book will be a little different from most stress-management tools on the market today. While most stress solutions offer relief for symptoms in only one or two of these areas, this book will show you how all 5 areas are important, and a successful stress solution will touch on each of them.

By adopting a trusting, open and relaxed attitude, we'll bring something more of ourselves to relationships of all kinds. This books will take a look at dating and relationships without stress and worry, as well as ways to bring tranquility and balance into your home and family life. Again, this book is not about eradicating stress from your life forever. We'll end with a consideration of the *positive* side of negative thinking, and how we can use stress and worry to our advantage.

Other books by this author:

- The Minimalist Budget: A Practical Guide On How To Save Money, Spend Less And Live More With A Minimalist Lifestyle

- How To Stop Worrying and Start Living – What Other People Think Of Me Is None Of My Business: Learn Stress Management and How To Overcome Relationship Jealousy, Social Anxiety and Stop Being Insecure

- Mindful Eating: A Healthy, Balanced and Compassionate Way To Stop Overeating, How To Lose Weight and Get a Real Taste of Life by Eating Mindfully

- Self-Esteem for Kids – Every Parent's Greatest Gift: How To Raise Kids To Have Confidence In Themselves And Their Own Abilities

Printed in Great Britain
by Amazon.co.uk, Ltd.,
Marston Gate.